CUSTOMER LOYALTY

HOW TO RETAIN YOUR CUSTOMER BASE THROUGH LOYALTY

I0483203

ANTHONY EKANEM

ISBN 978-1-63997-439-9

Contents

Preface

Customer loyalty is the most critical element to retain within a business relationship. A lot of benefits can be derived from a well-established loyal customer base. Large sums of money are often allocated to advertising, mainly to gain a bigger market share of customers. However, with the availability of loyal customers, the expenditures on advertising can be used for other beneficial projects in the business.

CHAPTER ONE

How Important is Customer Loyalty?

Companies that have many loyal customers enjoy the advantage of directing their funds to a self-supporting system in which the company constantly delivers superior value and high-quality products or services. This creates a comfortable relationship necessary to keep the customers happy and loyal. There is also the added advantage of pre-existing customers. They consciously help to introduce friends and family to the products and services based on personal testimonies and enthusiasm.

Another importance of retaining high loyal customer base is the fact that companies can focus on providing good customer induction schemes. These arrangements contribute to a high-yielding customer base and therefore provide high profits by reducing the need to spend money on attracting potential but not necessarily worthwhile customers. Such schemes should, however, not take the place of excellent customer service.

Trust is very hard to achieve and even harder to maintain. Yet, with the right process in place, it is possible to build trust between both parties. This trust element will afterwards translate to converting casual customers into loyal ones. Thus, any complaints regarding the products or services should be addressed swiftly to the satisfaction of the customer. Organisations that take the complaints of customers seriously are generally the ones that have the highest loyal customer base.

CHAPTER TWO

Know Your Loyal Customers

Your ability to discern your position with regards to your customer loyalty proportion can be tricky if not practically impossible, sometimes. However, some tried and proven techniques can be used to achieve this objective.

The ability to retain your customers has its advantages, and understanding customers' sentiments is fundamental to achieving customer loyalty. As loyal customers are a good indicator of a profitable and consistently successful business endeavour, taking the time to focus on understanding the level of customers' loyalty is both prudent and beneficial, especially in the long term.

This understanding can help predict, to some extent, the relation between the potentially loyal customers and those who may not become loyal customers needed to keep the business going. By making this discovery, you can then take the necessary actions to prevent potential customers from being one-time consumers.

Here are some things you need to consider in trying to understand the customers' mindset:

1. Trying to gather the required data to assess the potential customers' reason for making the purchase or for showing an interest in the service or product offered.

2. Finding out if the customers would be willing or even happy to introduce the product or service to others.

3. Getting feedback on the level of satisfaction derived from using the product or service, or the lack of satisfaction.

Armed with the above knowledge and information, there should also be a proactive action to address any adverse feedback learnt.

With the information gained from the customers, there should be concerted efforts to improve the products or services to further boost the commitment on the part of the customers to remain loyal.

CHAPTER THREE

Know Your Customers and Their Needs

To some extent, perceptions are made based on the knowledge gathered through specific methods. However, some of these methods may not be reliable, thereby creating the possibility of ineffective treatment of any complaints or needs that may arise. For a product or service to be successful and sustain itself, there is a compelling need to understand your target market and their peculiar needs.

The goal of understanding is to successfully eliminate possible wastage of efforts and resources on any wrong perceptions. Knowing the difference between the needs of the target market and measuring them against the perceived needs that you have been made to understand will help you to finetune your product or service to meet the needs of your customers. Sometimes, however, such information can be very difficult to process as the customers may not know what they need or want. This can be considered an advantage on your part as it creates the opportunity to promote your products or services to your customers in an attractive manner.

Also, when the customers' needs are clearly understood, there can then be a more straightforward method to garner customers' interest and successful sales. Advertising can be specifically designed to attract the customer based on the information learnt.

Continuously adapting to customers' interests will improve your customer loyalty success rate. This can contribute further to creating customers' faith in the products or services being offered as it shows your commitment levels and your willingness to ensure that your customers are happy.

All these points are intended to address the customers' numerous needs and interests.

CHAPTER FOUR

Provide Quality Products or Services

The key to identifying and creating products or services that will be well received by potential consumers lies in understanding their needs both on the conscious and subconscious levels. As many people do not know what their needs and wants are, the best-designed advertising can be used to trigger the desire for a product or service. As a business person, it is your job to identify and nurture the needs of your potential consumers. Researching products or services that are worth the customers' attention will yield the desired results.

It would be prudent never to underestimate or disregard any customer sentiments as this will eventually cause the customer to look elsewhere for their needs. Once relevant data is gathered, you should shift your focus to searching and presenting products that would be worthwhile and interesting to the potential consumers. When such products or services are identified, the potential or targeted consumers should then be wooed to buy the product or service.

Your products should always be of high quality as this is often the deciding factor on the customers' behalf between staying loyal and buying randomly. Another important consideration should be to continually provide the customer with updated and better versions of your products or services in keeping with the current times and requirements that may arise. Innovative products are usually well received by the market.

CHAPTER FIVE

Provide Exceptional Customer Service

A lot of businesses today offer similar products and services. Therefore, the main way you can have an edge over your competition is always to provide exceptional customer service.

Products today do not vary too much in terms of functions and price ranges; thus, by taking the trouble to provide good customer service, the customer can be persuaded to consider making repeat purchases.

Below are some recommendations you can follow in the quest to provide exceptional customer service:

1. As most initial enquiries are made over the phone, making it a habit to return or respond to all phone communications is very important and advisable. Doing so promptly is also another way you can make the customer feel important.

2. Providing a follow-up service or enquiry into the satisfaction of the product or service helps you and your customer to gain vital information and build a relationship of trust and commitment. This also allows

insight into the expectations of the customer.

3. Being committed enough to go the extra mile is another important feature in practice. This diminishing quality often puts customers off, and when extended, the customer will be highly impressed.

4. Taking the customers' concerns seriously and taking the necessary steps to address their concerns is also another beneficial trait of exceptional customer service. This does not only relieve the customers' concerns but also speaks to your commitment to customer satisfaction.

5. Though sometimes very difficult indeed, there is a need to stay focused and view the problem from the customers' perspective. Whenever they are confronted with a problem, a customer can often make unrealistic claims and remarks, thus having a calm demeanour would help to defuse any potentially unpleasant situation.

CHAPTER SIX

Your Company's Vision

To work effectively towards the company's or organisation's corporate goal, all stakeholders need to share the company's vision. The vision should be clearly defined so that everyone in the organisation understands the direction the company is going. This makes it easy for everyone to work towards reaching the clearly defined corporate goal reflected through the company's vision.

Having a clearly defined and powerful vision for the company and ensuring it is thoroughly followed and reflected by all, helps to encourage everyone to incorporate the said vision into their everyday work life to produce the desired results.

The vision should be appealing and well thought out to nurture the feeling of comradeship in belonging to something larger and better than oneself. It is also what drives people to reach their full potentials because of the excitement it creates.

When the organisation's direction and purpose clearly define the vision, it will inspire loyalty and caring attitudes, which will be displayed and reflected in the unique strengths that bring about the positive attributes of the excited employees.

The company's vision can help employees to challenge themselves to reach higher goals and productivity. Through the development of an appropriate vision for the company, stakeholders will feel a sense of importance and appreciation, thereby continuing to strive to do their best both for themselves and the company.